Copyright © 2025 by Samantha Bl

CW01645603

Contents

1 Introduction to Pre-Nups

A pre-nuptial agreement, or prenup, is a legally binding contract signed by both prospective spouses before marriage. It outlines how assets and liabilities will be divided in the event of separation or divorce. Understanding this foundational concept is paramount. Unlike a hastily-written, emotionally-charged post-nuptial agreement, a prenup offers a calm, reasoned approach to protecting your financial interests. It's a proactive strategy, not a reactive one, allowing you to enter marriage with clear expectations and reduced potential conflict later.

The historical context of prenups reveals a fascinating evolution. Initially viewed with suspicion, even disdain, as instruments that prioritized money over love, their acceptance has significantly broadened. This shift reflects changing societal attitudes toward marriage and personal finances. Modern prenups are increasingly common among couples, regardless of their net worth, recognizing their utility in managing potential financial complexities inherent in any long-term relationship. This widespread adoption showcases the move away from traditional norms to more practical, legally sound financial planning within a marriage. The trend mirrors the increasing importance placed on individual financial autonomy and safeguarding personal assets, demonstrating a clear shift in expectations within marriage itself. This evolution challenges the formerly-held beliefs that prenups indicate a lack of trust, instead highlighting their role as a tool for transparent financial communication and planning, thereby promoting a more secure and equitable marriage.

Comprehensive asset disclosure is vital for a legally robust prenup. This involves meticulously detailing every asset, from real estate and investments to personal possessions and intellectual property. Failure to fully disclose assets can render the agreement unenforceable or open it up to legal challenges later. Transparency is key – both parties must honestly reveal their financial status. An independent valuation of significant assets is often recommended to avoid disputes concerning their worth. This level of transparency builds trust, preventing future misunderstandings. Consider seeking professional advice from financial advisors and legal professionals to ensure a complete and accurate inventory, ensuring the agreement is legally sound and provides an accurate reflection of the couple's combined financial situation.

Debt, too, demands careful consideration. Pre-existing debts are explicitly addressed in the agreement, clearly outlining responsibility for repayment. This prevents one party from becoming solely responsible for the other's pre-marital debts, protecting their individual financial wellbeing. This clarity prevents potentially bitter disputes about financial responsibility, ensuring the agreement accurately reflects each spouse's financial liabilities and obligations. The agreement should specifically detail both the nature and extent of each party's debt, providing a roadmap for how that debt is handled, who is responsible, and strategies for addressing its repayment.

Spousal support, often referred to as alimony, requires careful negotiation. The agreement can specify whether support will be provided, its duration, and its amount. This provision allows both parties to agree upon a fair arrangement that avoids protracted legal battles post-separation. Waiving spousal support is also an option, but it requires careful consideration and full understanding of potential consequences. Such waivers should only be undertaken after thorough legal counsel. It's imperative to understand the tax implications of any support arrangement to ensure compliance with relevant regulations and prevent unexpected financial burdens. Consulting with tax professionals alongside legal experts provides an informed approach, safeguarding the future financial security of both partners.

The distinction between separate and marital property is crucial. Separate property, acquired before the marriage or received as a gift or inheritance during the marriage, typically remains solely owned. Prenups often aim to protect separate assets from being divided in a divorce. This protection ensures the financial independence of each party, preserving individual assets accumulated before the marriage or received as gifts during the marriage. This provision safeguards a party's financial future, ensuring that they are not penalized for their financial planning prior to marriage. Effective safeguarding of these assets reduces the likelihood of contentious and protracted post-marriage financial disputes.

Legal requirements for valid prenups vary by jurisdiction. These agreements must meet specific legal standards to be considered legally binding. This involves ensuring compliance with applicable contract law principles, including capacity, consideration, and free will. The involvement of independent legal counsel for each party is highly recommended to guarantee fairness and legal compliance. This is important for the agreement to stand up to legal scrutiny. The process of ensuring compliance emphasizes the importance of seeking legal counsel to advise both parties and prepare a legally sound document, promoting a fair and just outcome for both parties involved.

Regular review is paramount. Financial circumstances change; a prenup should be updated to reflect significant life events like business ventures, inheritances, or major debt accumulation. This ensures the agreement remains relevant and fair throughout the marriage. This proactive approach keeps the agreement aligned with the ever-changing financial circumstances of both parties, thereby avoiding future conflict. Regular review is integral for preventing legal ambiguity, preserving financial equity, and maintaining a legally sound document.

1.1 Defining Pre-nuptial Agreements

A prenuptial agreement, or pre-nup, is a legally binding contract entered into by prospective spouses before their marriage. Its primary function is to define and regulate the ownership and division of assets and property should the marriage end in divorce or separation. Unlike a simple agreement, a pre-nup necessitates careful legal drafting to ensure its enforceability and clarity, preventing future disputes. It's not just a financial document; it's a comprehensive plan outlining the couple's financial expectations and protections.

These agreements are increasingly common, particularly among individuals with significant assets or complex financial situations. They offer a level of certainty and control over the financial aspects of a marriage, minimizing potential conflict down the line. However, it is crucial to approach the process with transparency and mutual understanding to ensure that the agreement is fair and reflects the wishes of both parties. A poorly drafted or coercive pre-nup can be challenged in court and deemed unenforceable.

The creation of a pre-nup involves a detailed process of asset identification and valuation. Each party must completely disclose all their assets, liabilities, and income. This includes everything from real estate and investments to bank accounts and retirement plans. An independent valuation of these assets may be necessary to ensure fairness and accuracy. This transparency is paramount; any attempt to conceal assets can severely compromise the validity of the agreement.

Importantly, a pre-nuptial agreement isn't just about protecting assets; it's also about managing expectations regarding spousal support or alimony. The agreement can specify the amount and duration of spousal support, if any, in the event of divorce. This pre-determination prevents contentious negotiations after separation, saving time, resources, and emotional distress. However, it's vital to remember that laws regarding spousal support vary by jurisdiction, impacting the enforceability of these provisions.

Furthermore, the agreement clearly distinguishes between separate and marital property. Separate property, owned by one spouse before the marriage or acquired during the marriage as a gift or inheritance, is generally protected from division. Marital property, acquired during the marriage through joint efforts, is typically subject to division based on the terms of the agreement or state law, in the absence of a pre-nuptial agreement. Careful articulation of this distinction is crucial for maintaining asset protection.

Beyond the financial aspects, a pre-nuptial agreement can also address other matters relevant to the marriage. This can include provisions regarding the division of debts incurred before or during the marriage, as well as clauses covering inheritance rights, and other pertinent issues. Legal counsel is essential to ensure the comprehensive nature and legal soundness of the agreement. A well-drafted agreement acts as a proactive measure to reduce the financial uncertainties associated with marriage dissolution.

While the focus is on financial security, a successful pre-nuptial agreement should not be approached as a demonstration of mistrust. Instead, it's a practical, and sometimes necessary, tool for creating a clear and transparent understanding of each partner's financial contributions and expectations within the marriage. Open communication and informed consent are essential for a pre-nuptial agreement to foster trust and provide a solid foundation for the marriage. Transparency and mutual respect are key components of successfully navigating this process.

The process of creating a pre-nuptial agreement should be approached thoughtfully and with full understanding of its implications. Both parties should seek independent legal advice to ensure that their rights are protected and that they fully understand the terms of the agreement. Rushing into the process or failing to adequately understand the details could lead to complications later. A strong pre-nup is not just a legal document but a collaborative effort to build a solid financial future. Remember, this legal protection is a forward-thinking measure, allowing couples to safeguard their future. It is fundamentally about fostering a clear understanding and laying the groundwork for a successful, financially secure partnership.

1.2 Historical Context

The concept of legally binding agreements preceding marriage isn't a recent invention; its roots stretch surprisingly far back. While the modern pre-nuptial agreement, with its sophisticated clauses and legal intricacies, is a relatively recent development, the underlying principle of protecting individual assets within a marital union has existed for centuries. Think of ancient Roman law, where dowries played a vital role, essentially acting as a form of pre-marital asset protection for the wife and her family. These dowries, meticulously documented, provided a level of financial security, even if the marriage dissolved. The intention, while perhaps not identical to the aims of a modern pre-nup, mirrors the core function: safeguarding financial interests.

Early forms of pre-nuptial arrangements weren't always formalized documents as we understand them today. Often, they involved verbal agreements, family negotiations, and customary practices, varying widely based on cultural and social norms. In many societies, the transfer of property or inheritance played a significant role in solidifying a marriage alliance, acting as a form of implicit pre-nuptial agreement. The legal recognition and enforcement of these agreements varied significantly, depending on the specific legal systems and social contexts. The lack of standardized legal frameworks meant that disputes could be complex and outcomes often uncertain.

The evolution toward formalized written agreements accelerated with the rise of modern legal systems. The shift toward codified laws and standardized contract principles greatly influenced the development of the pre-nuptial agreement as we recognize it now. However, even then, their acceptance and legal standing differed widely across jurisdictions. Some legal systems readily accepted pre-nuptial agreements as valid contracts, while others viewed them with skepticism, sometimes even outright rejecting them. The legal battles and evolving jurisprudence surrounding these agreements reflect a struggle between the desire to uphold individual autonomy in financial matters and the societal norms that traditionally emphasized the unity of marital assets.

During the 20th century, particularly in Western societies, prenuptial agreements experienced a surge in popularity, coinciding with increased female economic independence and changing societal attitudes towards marriage. This period saw a refinement of legal frameworks, providing clearer guidelines on the validity, enforceability, and scope of pre-nuptial agreements. The rise of complex financial instruments and greater wealth accumulation further fueled the demand for sophisticated legal protections within the marital context. Courts grappled with numerous cases, shaping the legal interpretations that define today's best practices.

The historical context underscores a crucial point: pre-nuptial agreements are not simply a modern invention catering to the wealthy. They represent a continuous evolution of strategies employed to safeguard individual financial interests within the context of marriage. While their form and legal frameworks have evolved significantly, the underlying principle of protecting individual assets before marriage remains consistent throughout history, showing an enduring need for such legal tools regardless of wealth, social status, or cultural background. Understanding this history provides context to the contemporary use and interpretation of pre-nuptial agreements. It highlights the ongoing negotiation between individual rights and societal expectations surrounding marriage and financial security within a marital union, reflecting societal shifts over time.

2 Asset Valuation & Disclosure

Accurate asset valuation is paramount to a fair and legally sound pre-nuptial agreement. Neglecting this crucial step can lead to significant disputes and legal battles later. Think of it as building a house on a shaky foundation – the whole structure is at risk. A thorough inventory is the cornerstone of this process.

Detailed records, including bank statements, investment portfolios, property deeds, and business valuations, are vital. Don't overlook seemingly insignificant assets; every item of value, from retirement accounts to collections of rare stamps, must be accounted for. Consider consulting with financial professionals to ensure complete and accurate reporting. Their expertise can provide invaluable insight, preventing future complications.

Several valuation methods exist, each suited to different types of assets. Real estate, for instance, typically requires a professional appraisal. Businesses need a detailed valuation considering factors like profitability, market share, and intangible assets like brand recognition. Securities are simpler, with their current market value easily determined. Consistency in the chosen valuation method across all assets is key. Remember that transparency fosters trust and fairness.

Full disclosure is not merely a suggestion; it's a legal necessity. Each party must honestly present their complete financial picture, includ-

ing assets, debts, and liabilities. Any attempt to conceal or misrepresent information can severely jeopardize the agreement's validity and render it unenforceable. The legal ramifications of non-disclosure can be significant, potentially resulting in costly litigation.
Consider utilizing a neutral third party, like a financial advisor or accountant, to verify the accuracy of the disclosed information. This independent verification provides an added layer of protection and reinforces the agreement's legitimacy. It also helps minimize the risk of future disputes arising from valuation disagreements. This process may seem meticulous, even tedious, but the peace of mind it provides far outweighs the effort invested.
A well-structured pre-nuptial agreement outlining asset valuation and disclosure methods protects both parties' financial interests. This thorough process, though potentially complex, is fundamentally important to the overall success and durability of the agreement. This proactive approach minimizes potential conflict and promotes financial transparency, solidifying the foundation for a stable and equitable marital partnership. The careful documentation and verification steps contribute to a fair and legally defensible agreement, securing the financial well-being of both individuals involved. Remember, the goal isn't just to create a document; it's to create a secure financial framework for the future.

2.1 Comprehensive Asset Inventory

A comprehensive asset inventory is the cornerstone of a robust pre-nuptial agreement. Without a meticulous and detailed account of each party's assets, the agreement lacks a solid foundation, potentially leading to disputes and legal challenges down the line. This process requires meticulous attention to detail and, ideally, the assistance of financial professionals. It's not just about listing what you own; it's about accurately assessing its value.

Consider, for example, a family-owned business. Its valuation isn't a simple matter of looking at the bank balance. It requires a thorough appraisal considering factors such as profitability, market value, future growth potential, and even intangible assets like brand recognition. Similarly, real estate requires professional assessment, beyond simply citing the purchase price; location, current market conditions, and property improvements all impact its true worth. Ignoring these nuances can severely undervalue significant assets, creating potential problems later on.

Investments, whether stocks, bonds, or mutual funds, require careful valuation using current market prices or, in the case of more complex investment vehicles, professional appraisal. Don't overlook retirement accounts—401(k)s, IRAs, and pensions—as these often represent substantial assets. Precise figures, including current balances and projected future values (where possible), are crucial. The process shouldn't be rushed; thoroughness is paramount.

Beyond tangible assets, intellectual property rights deserve careful consideration. Patents, copyrights, trademarks, and business methodologies all hold potential value. Accurate valuation often requires specialized expertise and may depend on anticipated future income streams. Similarly, collections – whether stamps, art, or antique cars – require professional appraisal to determine their current market value, based on factors such as rarity, condition, and provenance. Accurate reporting of such items is essential.

Personal property is often overlooked, yet it can significantly impact the overall asset picture. Furnishings, jewelry, vehicles, and other personal belongings should be accurately cataloged, and their estimated value included. While not always easy to value precisely, a reasonable estimation, supported by documentation like purchase receipts or appraisals where available, is necessary. The goal is complete transparency.

Debt, often a less glamorous aspect of personal finance, is just as important to document. Outstanding mortgages, loans, credit card balances, and other liabilities must be comprehensively disclosed. Including detailed information such as interest rates, outstanding principal, and monthly payments ensures clarity for both parties. This transparency is essential for determining each party's net worth accurately.

Bank accounts, both checking and savings, are relatively easy to document, requiring only a recent statement. However, ensure all accounts are included, even those jointly held with others, or with little current balance. Transparency across all assets, regardless of size, is vital for the validity and future effectiveness of the agreement. This ensures clarity in financial matters.

In addition to these specific asset categories, ensure you document any other assets, however insignificant they may seem. This commitment to comprehensive listing demonstrates the seriousness with which both parties approach the agreement. Don't underestimate the importance of complete disclosure; failure to disclose assets accurately can lead to serious legal complications later. Remember, honesty and accuracy are paramount throughout the process.

Remember, the goal is to create a complete and accurate snapshot of your financial situation at the time of the agreement. This detailed inventory not only forms the basis of the pre-nuptial agreement but also provides a foundation for equitable discussions and potential future agreements should circumstances change. It's a critical step, but a necessary one, in safeguarding your financial future. This process requires time and effort, but the long-term benefits are well worth the investment.

The process of creating a comprehensive asset inventory should be approached with equal parts seriousness and practicality. While complete accuracy is the ultimate goal, understand that perfect precision is not always attainable, especially when dealing with assets like businesses or collections that are subject to market fluctuations. Focus on the principles of thoroughness, transparency, and fairness. The agreement isn't just a legal document; it's a reflection of the trust and understanding between two people embarking on a significant life commitment.

2.2 Valuation Methods

Accurate valuation is paramount in crafting a robust prenuptial agreement. Without it, the agreement becomes vulnerable, potentially leading to protracted and expensive legal battles down the line. Consider the implications of a poorly valued business interest, for instance, or an undervalued piece of real estate—these discrepancies can unravel the entire agreement. Therefore, thorough and professional valuations are essential.

Different asset types require different valuation approaches. Real estate is typically appraised by a licensed professional who considers location, size, condition, and comparable sales. Stocks and bonds are valued using their current market price, readily accessible through financial websites or brokers. Businesses, however, present a more complex challenge. Their valuation might involve a discounted cash flow analysis, an assessment of their assets and liabilities, or even a market-based approach considering comparable sales of similar companies. Each method has its own intricacies and requires expertise.

For intellectual property, the challenge of valuation increases. Patents, trademarks, and copyrights aren't always easily quantifiable in terms of direct market value. Their potential future earnings are often considered, factoring in licensing agreements, potential product sales, or brand recognition. This process necessitates expertise in intellectual property valuation and often involves projections that are inherently uncertain. It underscores the need for careful consideration and potentially expert counsel.

Perhaps the most challenging aspect of valuation lies in closely held

businesses. These entities often lack readily available market data, making traditional methods less reliable. Here, a detailed analysis of financial statements, including revenues, expenses, and profitability, is crucial. Moreover, qualitative factors like management expertise, market position, and growth potential significantly impact the valuation. Engaging a qualified business valuation professional becomes essential to avoid under\item or overvaluing these complex assets.
Beyond tangible assets, one must also consider intangible assets like goodwill. Goodwill represents the value of a business's reputation, customer relationships, and brand recognition—elements not easily reflected in traditional financial statements. Valuing goodwill requires an understanding of industry benchmarks, customer loyalty programs, and brand perception—an expertise not readily available to laypeople. In the context of a prenuptial agreement, overlooking this asset could result in a significant disparity.
The valuation process isn't just about assigning a dollar figure; it's about establishing transparency and building trust between the parties. Open communication and access to relevant documentation are critical. Both parties should understand the methodology used, feel comfortable with the results, and ideally, agree on the valuations before finalizing the agreement. This collaborative process helps to mitigate potential disputes and reinforces the prenuptial agreement's integrity. Remember, a contentious valuation process can easily overshadow the entire purpose of the prenuptial agreement.
Failure to accurately value assets can lead to serious consequences. A significant undervaluation could render the agreement unfair, making it more susceptible to legal challenges in the event of a divorce. Conversely, overvaluation can create an inflated sense of security, potentially leading to disappointment and conflict later. The importance of an unbiased and accurate valuation cannot be overstated. This step sets the foundation for a fair and legally sound prenuptial agreement.

The process, therefore, should be approached methodically. Start with a comprehensive inventory of all assets, including real estate, investments, businesses, and intellectual property. Then, research appropriate valuation methods based on the nature of each asset. It is highly advisable to obtain professional appraisals for complex assets, ensuring that the process is both meticulous and transparent. This ensures the valuations used are legally sound and withstand potential future scrutiny.

Furthermore, documentation is key. Maintain meticulous records of the valuation process, including supporting documents such as appraisals, market data, and financial statements. These documents not only demonstrate the thoroughness of the process but also serve as vital evidence should disputes arise later. This record-keeping is an important aspect of protecting both parties. Think of it as creating a detailed and verifiable history of the agreement's foundation.

In summary, accurate asset valuation is the cornerstone of a sound prenuptial agreement. The use of appropriate methods, professional expertise when necessary, transparent communication, and meticulous documentation are essential for creating a fair and legally defensible agreement. This process safeguards both parties' interests and helps prevent potential conflicts arising from inaccurate valuations. Don't underestimate the importance of this step—it truly is foundational to the agreement's success. The effort expended in this phase will offer considerable peace of mind and protection in the long run.

2.3 Transparency & Disclosure

Full and frank disclosure forms the bedrock of any legally sound pre-nuptial agreement. Without it, the entire agreement becomes vulnerable, potentially leading to protracted and costly legal battles down the line. Think of it as building a house on unstable ground; the foundation must be strong to withstand any storm. A lack of transparency introduces uncertainty and mistrust, undermining the very purpose of the agreement—to protect both parties' interests.

Complete transparency necessitates a comprehensive inventory of all assets. This isn't simply listing your house and car; it extends to bank accounts, investments (including retirement accounts and stocks), businesses, intellectual property rights, and even valuable collections. Nothing should be overlooked. Consider seeking professional advice from a financial advisor to ensure accurate valuations. Remember, the devil is in the details, and omitting even seemingly insignificant assets can severely jeopardize the agreement's validity.

Valuation is just as critical as identification. How you assess the worth of your assets significantly impacts the agreement's fairness and equity. Professional appraisals are often recommended, especially for complex or high-value assets like real estate or businesses. Using outdated or arbitrary valuation methods will only invite future disputes. Transparency here requires detailed documentation supporting each valuation. This might include appraisal reports, tax returns, and bank statements. The goal is not merely to list assets, but to demonstrably establish their worth in a way that stands up to legal scrutiny.

The process shouldn't feel like an adversarial game of financial disclosure. Open communication between both parties and their respective legal counsel fosters trust and reduces potential conflict. Remember, the pre-nuptial agreement is not about winning or losing; it's about collaboratively establishing a clear framework for managing finances during and after the marriage. Openness and honesty from both parties allow for a more collaborative process, increasing the likelihood of a well-structured and binding contract.

Moreover, consider the emotional implications of full disclosure. While transparency is paramount for legal validity, it also strengthens the relationship. By openly sharing your financial situation, you create a space for trust and mutual understanding. This proactive approach can even help both partners adjust expectations and plan their joint financial future. Openly disclosing debt is also crucial, as it avoids misunderstandings and ensures both partners are aware of their combined financial liabilities. Failing to do so can cause serious friction later and could invalidate the agreement.

This necessitates candid conversations about debt—student loans, credit card debt, mortgages, and any other outstanding financial obligations. It is not uncommon for one party to have significantly more debt than the other. Clearly outlining each party's debt responsibilities within the agreement protects both spouses. Failing to fully disclose pre-existing debts can later be used to invalidate the agreement. This is not about assigning blame; it's about creating an accurate financial picture.

The importance of professional guidance cannot be overstated. A qualified legal professional specializing in family law can not only guide you through the disclosure process but also ensure the agreement accurately reflects both parties' understanding and is compliant with relevant laws. Their expertise provides the reassurance that the agreement is legally sound and protects your interests. Independent legal counsel also helps mitigate potential biases, ensuring both parties receive fair treatment.

Finally, remember that the disclosure process is not a one-time event. Financial situations evolve, with assets fluctuating in value and debts being paid off or accumulated. Regular review and, if necessary, amendments to the pre-nuptial agreement are vital to ensure it continues to accurately reflect your shared financial reality. An outdated agreement is of little value; it's as good as having no agreement at all. Regular updates are an investment in your future, keeping the arrangement relevant, and legally sound. Consider annual reviews or whenever significant life changes affect your finances.

3 Debt & Liability Considerations

Dealing with pre-existing debt is crucial when crafting a prenuptial agreement. It's not about avoiding responsibility; rather, it's about clarity and protection. Failing to address this upfront can lead to significant complications later, potentially unraveling the entire agreement. Open and honest communication regarding each party's financial history is paramount. This includes credit card debt, student loans, business liabilities, and any outstanding judgments.

Transparency is key. Detailed documentation, such as credit reports and loan statements, should be provided. This isn't about judgment; it's about providing a complete financial picture to ensure a fair and equitable agreement. The agreement should explicitly state how each party's pre-marital debt will be handled. Will it remain solely the responsibility of the individual who incurred it? Or will there be some form of joint responsibility, perhaps in the event of a shared asset being used to consolidate debt? These questions require careful consideration and precise legal language.

Consider the impact of joint accounts opened before the marriage. Often, these represent a blending of finances, blurring the lines of individual responsibility for pre-existing debt. A well-drafted prenuptial agreement will clearly delineate the ownership and responsibility for these funds. Similarly, debts incurred jointly during the marriage will need distinct consideration. These debts might be handled differently than individual pre-marital debts, potentially requiring a more nuanced approach.

Furthermore, the agreement needs to define what constitutes a "pre-marital debt." There may be grey areas where determining the precise timeline is difficult. For instance, if someone secured a loan just weeks before the wedding, does it qualify as pre-marital or marital debt? Such ambiguities must be clarified, leaving no room for future disputes. The prenup should include specific language addressing such scenarios, perhaps using a clear cut-off date before the marriage.

Liability protection is another significant aspect. This goes beyond personal debts to encompass potential legal responsibilities. If one party is involved in a lawsuit, the agreement should address how this potential liability might affect the marital assets. Similarly, it should clarify the extent of liability each partner will assume for pre-existing business obligations. Business ownership can complicate matters significantly and needs a thorough approach. Ideally, separate business entities should be established to clearly define each party's stake in various entities.

A carefully crafted prenuptial agreement can provide valuable protection against unforeseen financial circumstances. It allows each party to enter the marriage with a clear understanding of their individual financial responsibilities, protecting their assets from potentially substantial financial risks. However, it's vital to remember that a prenuptial agreement isn't a substitute for responsible financial management. It's a tool for protection, not a license for reckless behavior.

Remember, seeking legal counsel is not an optional step. An experienced family law attorney can help navigate the complexities of debt and liability, ensuring that the agreement is legally sound and protects your interests effectively. They can guide you through the legal

nuances, helping you draft language that accurately reflects your intentions and withstands potential legal challenges.
Don't underestimate the importance of thoroughness. Any omissions or ambiguities in the agreement could leave you vulnerable to financial hardship. A detailed and precise document, crafted by a skilled professional, offers the best assurance of protecting your assets and ensuring a fair and equitable division of financial responsibilities. Neglecting this crucial step might prove costly in the long run.
The process of creating a prenuptial agreement is a collaborative one. Open communication, mutual understanding, and a commitment to transparency are vital for a successful and fair outcome. It's about building a foundation of trust and financial stability for the future, acknowledging the potential complexities of financial matters within a marriage. The legal framework must mirror this collaborative approach, working as a tool to protect, not to divide. A well-structured prenuptial agreement, therefore, should serve as a symbol of mutual respect and forward-looking financial planning.

3.1 Pre-marital Debts

Existing debts significantly impact pre-nuptial agreements. Understanding how these debts are handled is crucial for both parties. A well-drafted agreement clearly outlines responsibility for pre-marital debt, protecting each spouse's assets from the other's financial burdens. Failure to address this can lead to significant disputes later.
Consider John and Mary. John entered the marriage with substantial student loan debt. Mary, conversely, had no debts. Their pre-nuptial agreement could stipulate that John remains solely responsible for his student loans. This means Mary's assets—her inherited property, for example—would remain protected from creditors should John default. This protection safeguards Mary's financial independence and security. Conversely, a poorly worded agreement might jeopardize

both parties.

The process of addressing pre-existing debts needs meticulous attention to detail. It requires a thorough inventory of each party's liabilities, including credit card debt, loans, tax liens, and other financial obligations. Accurate documentation of these debts is essential, not only for the agreement itself but also to demonstrate transparency and good faith. Any omission or misrepresentation can severely undermine the agreement's validity, potentially resulting in court challenges. It's imperative to seek professional legal guidance for this process.

Beyond the specific debts, the agreement needs to address how these debts are to be managed during the marriage. Will one spouse assume responsibility for paying down certain debts? Will joint accounts be used to manage debt repayment? Will both parties contribute to debt repayment, and, crucially, in what proportions? These practical considerations must be explicitly laid out to avoid future conflict. Ignoring these practical details risks leaving the agreement vulnerable to challenges in court. Think of it as creating a financial road map for the marriage, outlining who is responsible for navigating the pre-existing financial terrain.

Furthermore, the agreement should specify how assets are protected from creditors in case of debt default. A key objective is shielding the non-debtor spouse's assets from claims by creditors. This involves not only identifying assets but also devising strategies for their protection. This might involve holding certain assets in separate trusts, using specific ownership structures, or creating other legal safeguards. In John and Mary's situation, this might entail maintaining Mary's inheritance in a trust to protect it from John's creditors.

Legal advice is essential. Negotiating these complex financial arrangements alone is ill-advised. A lawyer specializing in family law can provide expert guidance, ensuring the agreement is legally sound, comprehensive, and protects both parties' interests. They can also navigate the intricacies of state laws regarding debt and asset protection within marriage, which can vary significantly. The cost of legal advice is a small price to pay for the security and peace of mind that a well-crafted pre-nuptial agreement provides.

The role of transparency cannot be overstated. Both parties must provide full and honest disclosure of their financial situation, including all debts and assets. Hiding or minimizing debts can render the agreement unenforceable, leaving both parties vulnerable. Open communication about finances forms the bedrock of a strong and legally secure pre-nuptial agreement. This ensures fairness and promotes the long-term success of the agreement, providing a stable foundation for the marriage. It's about building trust and establishing clear expectations from the outset, setting a positive tone for the marriage.

Finally, review the agreement periodically. Financial circumstances change over time; job losses, unexpected inheritance, or substantial debt increase are all possibilities. Regular reviews ensure the agreement remains relevant and continues to safeguard your assets. Amendments and updates should be made as needed to reflect these shifts, preserving the intended protection it was designed to provide. Think of it as regular maintenance for your financial safety net.

3.2 Liability Protection

Protecting yourself from pre-existing debts is paramount when crafting a prenuptial agreement. Consider this scenario: one partner enters the marriage with significant business liabilities, perhaps stemming from a prior entrepreneurial venture. Without specific clauses addressing this, a future divorce could expose the other spouse's assets to these debts, even if they were acquired after the marriage. A well-drafted agreement clearly delineates responsibility for pre-existing debts, preventing unintended consequences and safeguarding the financial well-being of each individual. This protection extends beyond personal debts; it also encompasses any ongoing business liabilities, mortgages, or other financial obligations that either party carries into the marriage. Remember, a successful prenup isn't just about protecting assets; it's about protecting the future financial stability of both individuals involved.

The language used in the liability protection section needs to be precise and unambiguous. Vague terms leave room for interpretation, increasing the risk of disputes and challenges in court. Every potential liability should be addressed explicitly, avoiding generalized statements. For instance, instead of saying "each party is responsible for their own debts," detail the specific debts, their amounts, and the expected repayment plans. This clarity minimizes ambiguity and strengthens the agreement's legal standing. Furthermore, consider including a clause detailing how future liabilities will be managed, ensuring the agreement remains relevant even if unforeseen circumstances arise during the marriage. Consulting with an experienced attorney ensures the language accurately reflects the intentions of both parties and withstands legal scrutiny.

Beyond existing debts, think about the potential for future liabilities. Accidents happen, lawsuits arise, and unforeseen circumstances can impact financial stability. Your prenuptial agreement should address potential future liabilities, protecting each party's assets from the consequences of unforeseen events. This could involve specifying how joint liabilities—like a shared mortgage—will be handled in case of separation or divorce. Equally important is addressing potential personal injury claims; if one spouse is involved in an accident leading to a significant financial liability, the agreement should clarify which party bears responsibility. A thorough consideration of potential future liabilities significantly enhances the protective power of your prenuptial agreement.

Protecting business interests is particularly critical for entrepreneurs or individuals with substantial business assets. Your prenuptial agreement should clearly outline how business assets, liabilities, and ownership are managed during the marriage and in the event of separation or divorce. This might include detailing specific business ownership percentages, outlining responsibilities for business debts, and establishing how business profits or losses will be allocated. If one partner owns a successful business before the marriage, the agreement should safeguard their ownership and protect it from claims by the other spouse in the event of a divorce. It's essential to provide for the division of business assets in a fair and equitable manner, avoiding unintended consequences that could severely impact one party's financial future. This necessitates professional valuation of the business to ensure transparency and fairness in the agreement.

The role of insurance in liability protection cannot be overlooked. Comprehensive insurance coverage—such as liability insurance for businesses, personal injury protection, and other relevant policies—can provide a significant safety net. Your prenuptial agreement should address how insurance policies contribute to liability protection. It might specify which party is responsible for maintaining specific insurance policies or how insurance payouts would be allocated in case of a covered event. The inclusion of this element in the agreement adds another layer of protection, ensuring that unexpected events do not lead to disproportionate financial burdens on one party. Remember that thorough insurance coverage can mitigate the financial risks associated with various liabilities, strengthening the overall protective capacity of your prenuptial agreement.

Careful planning and comprehensive legal advice are crucial for effective liability protection in a prenuptial agreement. Never underestimate the importance of consulting with a qualified attorney specializing in family law to ensure that the agreement is legally sound and fully protects your interests. A skilled lawyer will guide you through the intricacies of liability protection, ensuring that the language is unambiguous and comprehensive. They can help identify potential vulnerabilities and suggest strategies for mitigating risks. Remember, a prenuptial agreement is a legal document with significant consequences; professional legal guidance is essential to ensure it achieves its intended purpose of safeguarding your financial future. Investing in professional legal help is an investment in your financial security.

4 Spousal Support & Alimony

Spousal support, or alimony, is a significant aspect of pre-nuptial agreements. It often represents a complex area, requiring careful consideration and precise legal drafting to ensure the agreement withstands scrutiny. Understanding the factors affecting spousal support determinations is paramount. These factors can include the length of the marriage, each party's earning capacity, contributions to the marriage (both financial and non-financial), and the standard of living established during the marriage. A comprehensive pre-nuptial agreement will clearly address these variables, striving for fairness and predictability.

Many couples elect to include provisions for spousal support within their pre-nuptial agreement. This proactive approach can avoid future disputes and the often-expensive legal battles that accompany divorce proceedings when these matters are left unaddressed. However, it's crucial to remember that such agreements must be fairly negotiated and fully disclosed to both parties. Any attempt to use such agreements for unfair advantage will likely be challenged. The aim is to create a balanced agreement that reflects the couple's realities and protects their interests.

One key element is the ability to waive spousal support. This is a significant decision, and it necessitates careful consideration of potential future circumstances. Both parties must fully understand the implications of such a waiver. Experienced legal counsel is essential in this process, ensuring both individuals comprehend the long-term financial consequences. A poorly-drafted waiver, missing vital details or lacking proper disclosure, can lead to serious legal issues down the line, potentially rendering the entire agreement voidable. Thorough legal advice, then, is paramount in achieving a fair and legally sound waiver.

Modifying a spousal support agreement after it's been legally established requires demonstrating a significant change in circumstances. This usually involves substantial shifts in income, unexpected health issues, or unforeseen financial difficulties. Courts are hesitant to alter these agreements unless compelling reasons are presented. The pre-nuptial agreement should include a clearly defined process for seeking modification, detailing the required steps and documentation necessary to make a successful case. This preemptive measure helps to avoid costly and protracted litigation, should the need to adjust support arise.

Finally, consider the tax implications of spousal support. Payments made under a spousal support agreement are often tax deductible for the paying spouse and taxable income for the receiving spouse. This can significantly impact the overall financial picture. A well-drafted pre-nuptial agreement will explicitly address these tax considerations, potentially outlining specific strategies to minimize tax burdens for both parties. Ignoring tax ramifications can lead to unintended and potentially substantial financial repercussions. Therefore, it's crucial to consult with both legal and financial professionals to ensure the agreement fully accounts for these aspects. Failure to do so can cause significant financial disadvantages, undermining the purpose of the pre-nuptial agreement itself. This thoroughness ensures that the agreement protects both parties' financial interests in a comprehensive and legally sound manner. The importance of meticulous planning, clear articulation of terms, and engagement with experienced professionals cannot be overstated when dealing with this sensitive and financially consequential aspect of pre-nuptial agreements.

4.1 Defining Spousal Support

Spousal support, or alimony, is a critical element within pre-nuptial agreements. It represents financial support provided by one spouse to the other during or after the marriage's dissolution. Understanding its nuances is crucial for crafting a legally sound and equitable agreement. Unlike simple property division, spousal support addresses the economic disparity that might arise between spouses after a marriage ends, often considering factors like the duration of the marriage, the earning capacity of each spouse, and the contributions each made to the family's well-being. Therefore, precise and thoughtful inclusion in your pre-nuptial agreement is essential.

The definition of spousal support varies across jurisdictions. Some states might define it as temporary or rehabilitative, aiming to assist a spouse in regaining financial independence. Others may grant permanent support, designed to provide long-term financial stability, particularly if one spouse significantly sacrificed career opportunities to support the family. Understanding your jurisdiction's specific legal definitions is paramount. Consulting legal professionals experienced in family law in your state is recommended to ensure your agreement aligns with local statutes and precedents. Failure to understand this aspect can create significant complications later.

A well-drafted pre-nuptial agreement should clearly define the terms of any spousal support. This includes specifying the amount, duration, and payment schedule. Vague language can lead to disputes. For example, stating "reasonable support" instead of a concrete amount will invariably trigger conflict. Detailed financial provisions, including precise figures, payment methods, and escalation clauses for inflation, ensure clarity and minimize future uncertainties. Remember, your agreement is a legally binding contract, and ambiguous wording could significantly impact enforceability.

Factors influencing spousal support determinations are numerous and complex. These include the length of the marriage, each spouse's earning capacity and contribution to the marriage, the standard of living established during the marriage, the health of each spouse, and the presence of children. A significant disparity in earning potential often influences support awards. For instance, if one spouse had a thriving career before marriage and significantly contributed financially, while the other significantly reduced their earning potential to raise children, the court may decide on spousal support. Thoroughly consider these elements when negotiating your pre-nuptial agreement.

Many pre-nuptial agreements incorporate waivers of spousal support. This means that both parties agree to forego any claims to alimony in the event of a divorce. This requires careful consideration, as giving up your right to future support can have long-term financial consequences. While a waiver may be advantageous to one party, it can prove detrimental to the other if unforeseen circumstances arise, such as unexpected job loss or serious illness. Therefore, a thorough risk assessment is critical before agreeing to a waiver. It is a complex decision that requires very experienced legal counsel.

Modifying support agreements established within a pre-nuptial agreement is usually more difficult than modifying those ordered by a court. Such modifications often necessitate a mutual agreement between the parties or a significant change in circumstances that was unforeseen and not previously addressed in the contract. This underscores the significance of a clearly articulated agreement, encompassing possible future scenarios. Therefore, comprehensive legal guidance is crucial to anticipate and address potential future

uncertainties within the context of your spousal support provisions. Consider the long term, carefully.
Finally, understanding the tax implications of spousal support is crucial. In many jurisdictions, spousal support payments are tax-deductible for the paying spouse and taxable income for the receiving spouse. This can significantly impact the net financial impact of the agreement. Failure to consider these tax ramifications during the negotiation process can lead to unintended consequences and increased financial burden on one or both parties. Seek professional tax advice in addition to legal counsel to ensure you fully comprehend the implications. Your comprehensive pre-nuptial agreement must safeguard both your legal and financial interests.

4.2 Factors Affecting Support

The length of the marriage is undeniably a significant factor. Longer marriages often lead to greater interdependence and shared assets, potentially increasing the likelihood and amount of spousal support awarded. Conversely, shorter marriages may result in less extensive financial intertwining, making a support claim less likely or substantially reducing its duration. This is especially relevant when considering the potential for rehabilitation and return to self-sufficiency, a key factor courts often weigh. The shorter the marriage, the more likely the courts see a prompt return to financial independence as feasible. Careful consideration of this temporal element is therefore critical in drafting the agreement, ensuring terms reflect the realistic possibilities given the anticipated marital timeline.
Another crucial consideration is the relative financial contributions of each spouse. This encompasses not just income earned during the marriage but also pre-marital assets, inheritances, and debts. A spouse who has significantly contributed financially throughout the marriage, especially one who may have sacrificed career opportuni-

ties for family responsibilities, has a stronger argument for support. Conversely, a spouse with substantial pre-marital wealth or a high earning capacity might be expected to contribute a greater portion to spousal support, or even waive it entirely. Documentation of these financial contributions, including pay stubs, tax returns, and bank statements, is paramount to demonstrate the disparities and justify the terms agreed upon. Clear, detailed financial records are vital in building a watertight argument and preventing future disputes.

The standard of living established during the marriage significantly shapes the parameters of spousal support. A pre-nuptial agreement needs to address this by acknowledging the lifestyle enjoyed during the marriage and determining a reasonable level of support to maintain a comparable standard, at least for a transition period. This consideration avoids creating an undue hardship on either party. For instance, maintaining a luxury lifestyle during marriage may necessitate ongoing significant support payments, while a more modest lifestyle reduces the financial burden associated with spousal support. A clear articulation of this standard, with supporting evidence such as housing costs, transportation, and leisure activities, is crucial.

Health and employability are other major influencers. Illness or disability severely impacting a spouse's earning potential can dramatically alter the terms of support. Similarly, a spouse with limited job skills or opportunities may require longer-term support to achieve financial stability. Agreements should include contingencies for unexpected health issues, ensuring appropriate support provisions to cover potential medical costs and lost income. Providing clear definitions and triggers for altering spousal support in these situations, coupled with methods of assessing the need for such support, will greatly benefit both parties. This ensures the agreement adapts to unforeseen circumstances, thus mitigating potential future conflicts.

The presence of children and their needs significantly impact spousal support calculations. The custodial parent frequently requires additional financial resources for childcare, education, and other related expenses. Pre-nuptial agreements should directly address the financial implications of child-rearing, determining how these costs will be shared between the parties, even if the support is waived or minimized. It is important to distinguish clearly between support for the children and support for the spouse. The agreement should ideally include detailed provisions that outline contributions to child-related expenses, thus eliminating potential future disagreements over financial responsibilities toward children, thereby maintaining clarity and fostering an equitable outcome.

Finally, the intent and desires of both parties are paramount. While the above factors provide objective criteria, it's crucial to remember the agreement should reflect the mutual understanding and expectations of both parties. Even if circumstances suggest a certain support structure, if both spouses agree to waive or significantly limit support, that agreement holds weight. However, it is crucial that this mutual agreement be reached fully informed, with both parties having independent legal counsel. A clearly articulated statement reflecting the mutual intention, free from undue influence or coercion, ensures the agreement's legal soundness and prevents future disagreements based on differing interpretations of intent. This final element underlines the importance of transparency and open communication in crafting a pre-nuptial agreement that effectively safeguards the financial future of both individuals.

4.3 Waiver of Spousal Support

A waiver of spousal support within a prenuptial agreement is a powerful tool, allowing couples to define their financial futures with clarity and precision. It's not about avoiding responsibility or lacking empathy; rather, it's about proactively shaping a financial landscape that reflects each party's individual circumstances and future goals, fostering a realistic and stable foundation for the marriage. Think of it as a carefully crafted roadmap, guiding you both through potential future challenges.

Such a waiver should be approached with meticulous care, requiring a comprehensive understanding of its implications. Consider the potential long-term consequences. Significant life changes, unforeseen circumstances, or unexpected career shifts could impact a party's financial standing far beyond the initial agreement's scope. A poorly drafted waiver could leave one party vulnerable and without recourse.

To create a strong and defensible waiver, both spouses need independent legal counsel. This ensures that each party understands the legal ramifications and the agreement's full implications. The lawyers will explain the rights being relinquished and provide advice on whether the waiver is appropriate for their specific situation, and they may even suggest alternative solutions. Remember, this isn't a process to be rushed; thorough consideration is crucial.

Moreover, transparency is paramount. Full disclosure of all assets, liabilities, and income streams is non-negotiable. Concealing information, even inadvertently, can render the entire agreement invalid, negating the intended protection. The agreement needs to be based on a clear and accurate representation of each party's financial reality. This process demands honesty and a frank assessment of the current financial situation.

The language used in the waiver must be unambiguous and legally sound. Vague or ambiguous wording can be easily misinterpreted, potentially leading to future disputes and litigation. A skilled attorney can draft precise language that effectively addresses all the scenarios and contingencies that may arise during the marriage and its potential dissolution. Remember, legal precision is key to avoiding future problems.

Furthermore, the waiver should specify the circumstances under which it may be modified or revoked. Unexpected events, such as catastrophic illness or disability, could significantly impact a party's ability to support themselves. The agreement could potentially include provisions allowing for adjustments under unforeseen hardship, striking a balance between financial planning and unforeseen life events. The process of reviewing and updating the prenuptial agreement should be outlined to assure clarity.

Finally, the process of reviewing and updating the agreement is just as critical as its initial drafting. A well-structured agreement typically outlines procedures for periodic reviews and amendments, ensuring it remains relevant and reflective of the couple's ongoing circumstances. Regular reviews allow you to address any changes to your assets, liabilities or income streams ensuring the waiver continues to be suitable and equitable. This underscores the ongoing nature of financial planning within a marriage. This consistent and clear approach to review ensures the agreement remains a valuable and relevant tool. Ignoring the update and review process will render the waiver potentially invalid or ineffective.

This chapter highlights the importance of understanding the implications of a spousal support waiver. This proactive approach to financial planning within a prenuptial agreement must be implemented cautiously and with professional legal guidance. Remember, the goal isn't to avoid responsibility; it's to build a strong and resilient financial foundation for your marriage. Therefore, seeking legal advice from independent counsel and understanding the nuances of such an important contractual provision are vital to ensuring that the agreement will stand up to legal scrutiny should a marriage end. This carefully considered approach to financial planning is a testament to the commitment to a responsible and lasting partnership.

4.4 Modifying Support Agreements

Circumstances change. Jobs are lost, businesses boom, inheritances are received, and unforeseen health issues arise. These life events can significantly impact the financial landscape of a marriage, potentially rendering a pre-nuptial agreement outdated or inequitable. Therefore, understanding the process of modifying a support agreement is crucial. This is not about rewriting the entire agreement; it's about targeted adjustments to address specific, demonstrable changes.

Modifying a pre-nuptial agreement, especially the spousal support sections, requires a clear understanding of the legal framework governing such changes. Most jurisdictions allow for modification, but the grounds for modification are usually restricted to substantial and unforeseen changes in circumstances. A simple change in income, for instance, might not be sufficient. Think of a major, unexpected job loss that leaves one spouse facing financial hardship, or a debilitating illness requiring extensive medical care and loss of earning capacity. These are the kinds of situations that might justify a modification.

The process itself is typically initiated by filing a formal petition with the court. This petition needs to clearly and concisely articulate the reasons for seeking modification, providing substantial evidence to support the claim. Think of it as a legal argument, backed by financial statements, medical records, or other relevant documents. The court will then review the petition, considering the original agreement, the current circumstances, and applicable laws. This isn't a quick process; it often involves several court appearances, legal briefs, and negotiations.

Remember, your original agreement likely contains a clause addressing modifications. Carefully review this clause. It will likely outline the process, required documentation, and any specific conditions that must be met. Ignoring this clause can weaken your legal position. It could lead to the rejection of your modification request. Always seek legal counsel before initiating any modification proceedings. A skilled attorney specializing in family law can guide you through the process, ensuring your rights are protected and your arguments are presented effectively.

The success of a modification request hinges on proving a material and unexpected change in circumstances. It's not enough to simply state that things have changed; you need to demonstrate this change with concrete evidence. This might involve providing tax returns to show a significant decline in income, medical bills to illustrate unexpected healthcare costs, or employment records demonstrating job loss or a career change. The more comprehensive and convincing the evidence, the stronger your case will be.

Furthermore, the court will consider the original intent of the agreement. Were there specific provisions designed to address unforeseen circumstances? The judge will review the entire agreement, looking for clues about the parties' expectations and intentions. Understanding these implications from the beginning is vital. This highlights the importance of seeking professional legal advice during the creation of the pre-nuptial agreement to ensure it adequately addresses potential future scenarios and is drafted with clarity to allow flexibility for modification when needed.

Moreover, the court will also consider the fairness of the modification. Even if you prove a material change in circumstances, the court will not necessarily approve a modification that is deemed unfair to the other party. This requires a nuanced understanding of equitable principles and the judge's interpretation of fairness in the specific context of your case. The modification must strike a balance between addressing the hardship you're experiencing while still acknowledging the other spouse's interests.

Successfully modifying a spousal support agreement requires careful planning, meticulous documentation, and strong legal representation. It's not a process to be undertaken lightly. It's a legal battle requiring strategic thinking and persuasive argumentation, as each case is unique and hinges on the specifics of the circumstances. The importance of proactively seeking legal counsel cannot be overstated. They can guide you in gathering the necessary evidence, crafting a compelling legal argument, and navigating the complexities of family law. Remember, preserving financial stability for both parties remains the overarching goal, even amidst significant life changes. Therefore, working towards a mutually agreeable outcome, if possible, is always preferable to a lengthy and potentially costly court battle. Proactive communication and negotiation can facilitate a smoother and less contentious process. A collaborative approach, where both parties are actively involved in exploring solutions, can help preserve the relationship while addressing the need for modification.

4.5 Tax Implications of Support

Understanding the tax implications of spousal support within a prenuptial agreement is crucial for both parties. It's not merely a matter of legal semantics; the tax treatment directly impacts the financial realities of the agreement, potentially altering the overall economic distribution significantly. Failure to properly consider these implications can lead to unforeseen financial burdens and legal disputes down the line. Careful planning and professional advice are essential to avoid costly mistakes.

A key aspect to consider is the taxability of spousal support payments. Depending on the terms of the agreement and applicable tax laws, these payments may be deductible by the paying spouse and taxable as income for the receiving spouse. This is a common scenario, especially in agreements where a significant disparity in earning potential exists. The tax code's characterization of the payments greatly influences both parties' net income after taxes.

For example, an agreement specifying periodic payments labeled as "alimony" often follows the rules outlined in the Internal Revenue Code, subject to certain criteria. These criteria dictate conditions such as payment timelines and stipulations preventing the ex-spouses from living together. A crucial factor is the agreement's effective date, as tax rules have evolved, and older agreements might be subject to different provisions. If the agreement isn't correctly structured and designated under the appropriate tax codes, it could result in unexpected tax liabilities for one or both parties, possibly even leading to penalties.

Conversely, if the agreement includes a waiver of spousal support, the tax implications shift accordingly. This removes any tax deduction for the paying spouse and eliminates taxable income for the recipient. The decision to include such a waiver is significant and necessitates a thorough examination of the individuals' financial circumstances and long-term projections. While it might appear simpler from a taxation perspective, a poorly considered waiver can be financially detrimental in the long run, especially for the spouse forgoing potential support. Thorough financial modeling should be used to explore both scenarios.

The complexities don't end there; tax laws are not static. They are subject to change at the legislative level. Therefore, even a well-drafted agreement could become outdated, necessitating review and potential amendments to reflect the current tax laws. A prenuptial agreement isn't a 'set it and forget it' document; its relevance and effectiveness rely on regular review and adaptation, particularly when it includes substantial spousal support provisions. Ignoring these legal and financial dynamics could lead to significant and unexpected tax ramifications.

Furthermore, the interaction between state and federal tax laws presents yet another layer of complexity. Each jurisdiction has its own interpretation and specific provisions concerning the taxability of spousal support. This necessitates an understanding of both federal and state laws, particularly when the spouses reside in different states or if the agreement involves cross-state property distributions. Seeking the guidance of tax professionals familiar with the nuances of both federal and state laws is strongly advised to avoid any unintended tax liabilities or misunderstandings.

Therefore, the tax implications of spousal support in a prenuptial agreement are not simply incidental details but rather pivotal considerations affecting the long-term financial implications for each spouse. Professional legal and financial advice is paramount in navigating these complexities. Failure to comprehensively address the tax implications can undermine the effectiveness and fairness of the entire agreement. The importance of comprehensive planning and diligent professional guidance in crafting a robust and tax-efficient agreement cannot be overstated. Thorough preparation can avert potential legal and financial pitfalls. The consequences of negligence can be severe and long-lasting, impacting both parties' financial stability and security. Prioritizing this critical aspect protects both parties and ensures the overall success and lasting benefits of the prenuptial agreement.

5 Property Division & Ownership

Understanding the difference between separate and marital property is fundamental. Separate property encompasses assets owned solely by one spouse before the marriage, received as a gift or inheritance during the marriage, or acquired using only separate funds. This could include a house purchased before the wedding, an inherited painting, or a bank account funded solely with pre-marital savings. Conversely, marital property is anything acquired during the marriage through joint efforts, such as a jointly owned home purchased after the wedding, investments made with combined income, or even increases in the value of separate assets due to joint effort. Clearly defining these categories within your pre-nuptial agreement is critical for asset protection.

A pre-nuptial agreement offers a powerful tool for safeguarding your separate property. By explicitly outlining what constitutes separate property and declaring that it remains solely owned, you establish a clear legal boundary. For instance, if you owned a business before the marriage, your pre-nup can stipulate that its profits and assets remain yours, irrespective of marital income or expenditures. This prevents future disputes over the business's ownership and valuation during a potential divorce. The agreement must be precise; vague wording can be challenged in court, undermining the agreement's

protective measures.
Protecting your separate assets requires more than simply listing them; you must specify how they will be managed and protected during the marriage. This might involve maintaining separate bank accounts, ensuring transparent financial records, and perhaps even establishing a trust to hold certain assets. These measures create a clear separation of financial resources, reinforcing the pre-nup's provisions. For example, regularly reviewing and updating the list of assets in the agreement is crucial. Changes in investments, property values or new acquisitions should all be documented. Failure to do so can weaken the agreement's legal standing and compromise its effectiveness.
Furthermore, the agreement should specifically address how income generated from separate assets will be handled. For example, if your separate property generates income, the pre-nup can specify that this income remains separate property, unless otherwise agreed upon. This crucial detail prevents any confusion regarding the allocation of funds and strengthens the agreement's protective function. The specificity of this provision underscores the importance of seeking legal counsel to ensure the agreement clearly reflects your intentions and is enforceable under applicable law. Consulting a professional versed in pre-nuptial agreements will guide you through complex situations and ensure you understand the legal nuances involved.
Consider the situation where one spouse owns a significant family business. The pre-nup can explicitly state that this business is considered separate property and therefore not subject to division in a divorce. However, the agreement should also clarify whether any growth or profits generated from the business during the marriage will be considered separate or marital property. This necessitates meticulous consideration of the nuances of business ownership and accounting practices during the creation of your pre-nuptial agreement. Ambiguity in this area will likely lead to legal disputes. Thor-

ough and precise legal language will protect against any unforeseen challenges.
Finally, remember that a pre-nuptial agreement is not a static document; it's a living instrument that should adapt to evolving circumstances. Regular review and amendment are vital to maintain its relevance and efficacy. A substantial change in either spouse's financial standing, the acquisition of substantial new assets, or even a significant shift in the couple's life goals should trigger a reassessment of the agreement's provisions. Consulting legal counsel for periodic reviews ensures that the agreement remains a robust and reliable tool for protecting your assets and financial stability, providing a solid legal foundation for your future. This proactive approach prevents future complications and ensures the ongoing protection afforded by your pre-nuptial agreement. The goal is to maintain clarity and accuracy in your pre-nuptial agreement, reflecting the realities of your changing financial life.

5.1 Separate vs. Marital Property

Understanding the difference between separate and marital property is fundamental to crafting a robust pre-nuptial agreement. Separate property comprises assets owned solely by one spouse before the marriage, acquired during the marriage as a gift or inheritance, or explicitly designated as separate in the agreement itself. This includes things like inheritances, property purchased before the wedding, and even specific gifts received during the marriage from family members. Careful documentation is key; maintain clear records of purchase dates, ownership details, and any associated financial documentation.
Marital property, conversely, represents assets acquired by either or both spouses during the marriage, not as gifts or inheritances. This generally includes items purchased jointly, income earned during the

marriage, and assets that appreciate in value during the marriage. The distinction is crucial as separate property usually remains solely owned by the individual spouse, while marital property is often subject to equitable distribution in a divorce proceeding, unless explicitly addressed in a pre-nuptial agreement. Therefore, it's vital to delineate these categories clearly within your agreement.

Protecting your separate property requires specific and unambiguous language in the pre-nuptial agreement. Vague terms or omissions can lead to disputes and costly litigation. Each asset you wish to protect should be meticulously identified within the agreement, and the agreement should clearly state that these assets remain your separate property even in the event of a divorce. Furthermore, you should consider including a detailed description of the asset, its location, and its approximate value. This level of specificity helps minimize potential ambiguity. Remember, the more detail you provide in your pre-nup, the more secure your assets will be.

Defining separate property correctly avoids misunderstandings, ensuring that individual assets acquired before the marriage remain individually owned. It goes beyond simply listing possessions; it involves a careful accounting of financial accounts, investments, businesses, and other holdings. For instance, a family business owned before marriage would need explicit protection; any increase in its value during the marriage should be clarified as either separate or marital property within the agreement. The same meticulous approach is required for significant inheritances received during the marriage.

Beyond tangible assets, intellectual property rights, patents, copyrights, and any business interests deserve special attention. These often require specialized legal advice to ensure appropriate protection in a pre-nuptial agreement. The value of these assets can be difficult to assess, necessitating the involvement of qualified valuers and legal experts. It is also important to clearly outline the division of any future earnings derived from these assets. This aspect requires specific clauses to prevent conflicts.

The pre-nuptial agreement should include provisions addressing the management and disposition of separate property during the marriage. This helps manage expectations and prevent potential misunderstandings. It might stipulate that each spouse maintains independent control over their respective separate property, outlining how expenses related to separate assets are handled, for example, ensuring the upkeep of the family home if owned solely prior to marriage remains the responsibility of the sole owner.

Moreover, a pre-nuptial agreement can address scenarios where separate property becomes commingled—mixed with marital property. Careful planning will allow for a method of accounting for the commingling, perhaps by tracking each contribution independently to maintain the character of the separate property. This is complex and necessitates detailed financial records. Careful legal counsel is recommended to navigate these nuances effectively, minimizing the risk of disputes later.

Finally, anticipate future acquisitions. What if you inherit property during the marriage? Your pre-nuptial agreement needs to specify how such future acquisitions will be classified and protected. This forward-thinking approach will address potential scenarios that might otherwise create significant conflict in the future. By thoughtfully considering the various possibilities, and obtaining the right legal support, you can establish a clear, protected framework for your separate assets, ensuring financial stability even under the complex circumstances of a marriage dissolution.

5.2 Protecting Separate Assets

Protecting assets accumulated before marriage is paramount. A well-drafted pre-nuptial agreement acts as a shield, safeguarding these holdings from potential division in the event of divorce. This protection isn't just about financial security; it's about preserving the fruits of years of labor, inheritance, or gifts—things that hold sentimental value beyond monetary worth. Think of the family heirloom, the business built from the ground up, or the property gifted by a beloved grandparent; these are frequently among the most important and should be specifically addressed.

Understanding the distinction between separate and marital property is fundamental. Separate property encompasses assets owned before the marriage, received as gifts or inheritance during the marriage, or acquired through separate efforts during the marriage (excluding income commingled with marital funds). This is often overlooked by individuals entering into a pre-nup. Each asset should be clearly identified within the agreement; a simple list is insufficient. Comprehensive descriptions and appropriate valuation methods, as detailed in previous chapters, ensure clarity and reduce future conflict.

The agreement should explicitly state that all such separate assets remain the exclusive property of the owner, free from division or claims during separation or divorce. This necessitates a meticulous approach to documentation; gather all relevant documents like deeds, titles, bank statements, and business valuations. Failing to do so leaves the pre-nup vulnerable to legal challenges. Consider independent professional appraisals to counter any potential disputes on asset valuation. Remember, these documents serve as your primary defense should any dispute arise.

Consider including clauses that address future acquisitions of separate property. For instance, if one spouse receives an inheritance during the marriage, the agreement should explicitly state that this remains their separate property. Similarly, if one spouse continues to build their pre-marital business, its growth and associated assets remain solely theirs. Including such specifics greatly strengthens the agreement's ability to safeguard your assets.

Furthermore, the agreement must clearly define the means by which separate property will be maintained. This could involve designating separate bank accounts, investment accounts, or even business entities. Keeping such assets strictly separate reduces the risk of them becoming entangled with marital property, and even helps to reduce any potential ambiguity in the event of separation. Maintaining meticulous financial records is key to proving the separate nature of the assets, and this must be reflected in the agreement's text.

Don't underestimate the importance of legal counsel. Navigating the complexities of pre-nuptial agreements requires experienced legal professionals. They can help you craft an agreement that protects your separate assets effectively and ensures its enforceability within your jurisdiction. Attorneys also provide crucial advice on the legalities involved and guide you to avoid potential loopholes which might weaken your agreement. This is not just a financial decision, it is a legal commitment that needs careful consideration.

The process may feel intimidating, but remember it's a preventative measure designed to secure your future. It's about protecting not only financial assets but also the emotional security tied to them. A well-structured agreement offers peace of mind, knowing that your hard-earned possessions, and irreplaceable heirlooms are legally protected, regardless of how your marriage turns out. Investing the time and resources into crafting a robust agreement now can save you considerable stress and legal expenses in the future. Remember to review the agreement periodically to ensure it remains up-to-date with your changing financial circumstances. This proactive approach guarantees your separate assets are fully protected throughout your marriage.

6 Legal Considerations & Enforcement

Legal requirements for a valid pre-nuptial agreement vary by jurisdiction, but generally involve several key elements. These agreements must be entered into voluntarily, without duress or coercion. Both parties must have full disclosure of their assets and liabilities, and it must be clear that each party understands the terms. Independent legal counsel is strongly recommended for each party, ensuring each understands the implications of the agreement before signing. A poorly drafted or improperly executed pre-nuptial agreement could be challenged in court, potentially leading to its invalidity. Therefore, seeking professional legal advice is crucial for a successful and legally sound outcome.

The principles of contract law underpin the validity and enforceability of pre-nuptial agreements. These agreements are essentially contracts, binding both parties to the terms they agreed upon. Fundamental aspects of contract law, such as offer, acceptance, consideration, and capacity, must be satisfied. A lack of consideration, for instance, where one party receives no benefit from the agreement, could render the agreement invalid. Similarly, if one party lacked the mental capacity to understand the terms of the contract at the time of signing, it could be deemed unenforceable. These are critical points to remember.

Should disagreements arise concerning the terms of the pre-nuptial agreement, several dispute resolution mechanisms are available. Mediation offers a less adversarial approach, facilitating communication and compromise between the parties. Mediation helps to maintain a collaborative atmosphere, potentially reducing legal costs and emotional stress. However, if mediation fails to resolve the dispute, arbitration, a more formal process with a neutral third-party arbitrator rendering a binding decision, is an option. Ultimately, if all other methods fail, litigation – pursuing the matter through the court system – is a final resort. Litigation is the most expensive and time-consuming option, frequently emotionally draining for all involved.

Enforceability of a pre-nuptial agreement hinges on several factors. Courts generally uphold agreements that are fair and equitable, reflecting a reasonable understanding of each party's financial situation. Agreements considered unconscionable, meaning grossly unfair to one party, may be overturned. The level of disclosure plays a crucial role. Lack of full and transparent disclosure can provide grounds for challenging the agreement's validity. Further, proving undue influence or coercion exerted upon one party during the negotiation process can lead to the agreement being declared invalid. Therefore, creating a fair and transparent agreement is paramount.

The legal landscape surrounding pre-nuptial agreements is complex and varies across jurisdictions. State laws significantly influence the requirements and enforceability of these agreements. Understanding these jurisdictional differences is paramount, as the validity and interpretation of the agreement can vary considerably. For example, some states have stricter requirements for disclosure or may be less inclined to enforce certain provisions compared to others. Therefore, seeking legal advice specific to your jurisdiction is critical to protecting your interests.

Navigating the legal complexities of pre-nuptial agreements demands professional guidance. Engaging experienced legal counsel well in advance of the wedding ensures a thorough understanding of the relevant laws and the crafting of a legally sound and protective agreement. Attorneys specializing in family law are best equipped to handle these matters, as they possess specific expertise in this area. Their guidance safeguards both parties' interests and minimizes the risk of future legal disputes. They offer vital insights into drafting clauses specific to various situations.

While pre-nuptial agreements cannot cover every possible scenario, they offer a significant framework for financial security and protection before marriage. They also act as a preventative measure, clarifying expectations and avoiding potential conflicts over assets and support, particularly if the relationship ends. Despite this, they are not a guarantee against all future disputes. Unforeseen circumstances or situations not adequately addressed within the agreement can still lead to legal challenges. However, a well-drafted agreement significantly minimizes these possibilities.

Remember, a pre-nuptial agreement is not designed to prevent love and commitment but rather to safeguard both parties' financial well-being should the marriage not succeed. By providing a legally sound structure to address financial matters, pre-nuptial agreements facilitate open communication and transparent discussions, enhancing the relationship's foundation. Therefore, a pre-nuptial agreement can be considered a responsible and forward-thinking approach to protecting one's financial future, even within a loving and committed partnership. While it might seem counterintuitive, it promotes a healthy discussion of financial realities.

6.1 Legal Requirements

Creating a legally sound pre-nuptial agreement requires meticulous attention to detail and adherence to specific legal requirements. Failure to meet these standards can render the agreement unenforceable, leaving you vulnerable to potentially unfavorable outcomes in the event of a separation or divorce. The consequences of an invalid agreement can be far-reaching, impacting your financial security and future well-being.

First and foremost, the agreement must be entered into voluntarily. Coercion, undue influence, or duress of any kind will invalidate the agreement. Both parties must have full and independent legal representation, ensuring that their interests are adequately protected throughout the negotiation and signing process. This ensures each party understands the implications of the agreement, preventing future disputes arising from a lack of comprehension. A simple acknowledgement signed by each party isn't sufficient; active participation guided by individual legal counsel is critical.

Secondly, full and complete disclosure of all assets and liabilities is paramount. This involves a thorough inventory of all personal property, real estate holdings, business interests, investments, debts, and any other financial obligations. Imprecise, incomplete, or intentionally misleading disclosure can be grounds for challenging the agreement in court. Independent valuation of assets by qualified professionals further bolsters the agreement's legitimacy, supporting the accuracy of declared financial information. Think of it as a comprehensive financial snapshot of your life taken before the marriage. This transparent approach builds a solid foundation of trust and fairness.

The language used within the agreement must be clear, unambiguous, and readily comprehensible. Vague or overly complex wording leaves room for interpretation and potential disputes. Legal jargon should be avoided wherever possible, ensuring that both parties understand the exact terms and conditions. Using simple, direct language minimizes the likelihood of misinterpretations, providing clarity in what would otherwise be an emotionally charged situation. This promotes a thorough understanding and contributes to its overall legal soundness.

Finally, the agreement must comply with all applicable state and/or federal laws. Requirements vary by jurisdiction, with certain stipulations regarding spousal support, property division, and other related matters. It's essential to consult with an attorney experienced in family law to ensure that the agreement aligns with the current legal framework in your state of residence. Failing to do so can render the agreement ineffective, jeopardizing the protections it was designed to provide. Ignoring jurisdictional specifics could have serious repercussions.

The timing of the agreement's execution also merits attention. While there's no single "best" time, it is generally advisable to complete the process well before the wedding date, allowing sufficient time for negotiations, legal review, and any necessary revisions. Rushing the process can lead to hastily drafted provisions and unintended consequences. Adequate time ensures a thorough review, minimizing the potential for omissions or errors that could compromise the agreement. This allows for measured decision-making, prioritizing careful consideration over rushed action.

Moreover, it's crucial to remember that a pre-nuptial agreement isn't a static document. As circumstances change — a significant inheritance, a career change, or the birth of children — review and potential amendments may be necessary. This ensures that the agreement continues to reflect the parties' current financial situations and objectives. Regular revisits ensure continued relevance and maintain the protection intended for both parties. It's a tool to help manage a dynamic life, not a rigid and unchanging contract.

In conclusion, navigating the legal requirements of creating a prenuptial agreement demands careful planning and professional guidance. Addressing each requirement meticulously contributes to a legally sound and enforceable agreement, providing valuable protection for your financial future. Remember, the goal is to foster clarity, fairness, and transparency throughout the process, ensuring that your pre-nuptial agreement effectively safeguards your interests. This thorough approach safeguards against misunderstandings and future legal complications, protecting your assets and promoting financial stability.

6.2 Contract Law Principles

Understanding contract law is fundamental to the validity and enforceability of any prenuptial agreement. A prenup, at its core, is a legally binding contract, subject to the same principles governing all contracts. Therefore, a thorough grasp of these principles is crucial for both parties involved.

To be legally sound, a prenuptial agreement must meet several key requirements. First, it must demonstrate mutual consent, meaning both parties voluntarily enter the agreement without coercion or undue influence. Evidence of duress, for example, whether subtle or overt, could invalidate the entire agreement. This means each party must have a full and complete understanding of what they're agreeing to, with no pressure to sign. Consider the implications of unequal bargaining power, such as a significant wealth disparity between the individuals. Such circumstances need careful scrutiny to ensure the process is genuinely fair and consensual. Furthermore, the process should be transparent, allowing independent legal counsel for each party to help in understanding the implications of the document.

Next, consideration must exist. This means each party must receive something of value in exchange for their commitments. It doesn't necessarily mean an equal exchange of assets; rather, it indicates a mutual exchange of promises. One party might relinquish potential claims to certain assets in exchange for financial security or other stipulations detailed in the agreement. This exchange, however slight, is considered sufficient to satisfy the consideration requirement. The essence is that the agreement is not merely a one-sided arrangement. The fairness of the consideration given will be evaluated should the agreement come under legal scrutiny.

Furthermore, the agreement's terms must be clear, unambiguous, and specific. Vague language or ambiguous phrasing can be the source of significant disputes later. Terms related to asset division, spousal support, and debt allocation should be defined precisely. Avoid generalized or overly broad terms. Specific dollar amounts, percentages, or descriptions of assets are strongly recommended. It is imperative to use legally sound language and avoid colloquial terms or jargon that could be misinterpreted. The detail needed prevents the later unraveling of the agreement over points that were not explicitly discussed. Additionally, the entire agreement should be reviewed by legal professionals to ensure complete clarity and eliminate potential loopholes that could be exploited in the future.

Legality is another crucial aspect. The agreement must adhere to all relevant laws and regulations, reflecting the jurisdictions involved. Illegal provisions, such as those that violate public policy or attempt to limit child support or custody rights, are unenforceable. It's essential to engage legal professionals familiar with family law in your specific jurisdiction to ensure the agreement's legality and compliance with all applicable statutes. This ensures the agreement is upheld in a court of law and its provisions are correctly interpreted. In the case of agreements spanning across multiple jurisdictions, thorough legal review is even more vital due to differing legal regulations across state and international lines. This complex interplay of legal frameworks needs careful management to avoid inconsistencies and potential conflicts.

Finally, capacity is a critical element. Both parties must possess the legal capacity to enter into a contract. This means they must be of legal age, of sound mind, and not under the influence of substances that impair their judgment. Any evidence suggesting a lack of capacity—whether at the time of signing or continuously throughout the agreement's lifespan—can render the contract voidable. It's crucial to ensure that both parties fully comprehend the agreement's implications. This consideration is especially critical when there are significant imbalances in power or when there are indications of potential coercion. Therefore, independent legal counsel for each party is highly recommended to confirm capacity and facilitate informed consent. This ensures that the agreement stands on a foundation of genuine agreement.

The enforceability of a prenuptial agreement heavily depends on whether these contractual principles are satisfied. A failure to meet these requirements can lead to the agreement being deemed invalid or unenforceable, leaving both parties vulnerable and potentially triggering lengthy and costly legal battles. Professional legal counsel is essential in ensuring your prenuptial agreement is comprehensive, legally sound, and designed to safeguard your financial interests in the long run. Therefore, the entire process must be approached with due diligence and careful consideration, and the advice of legal counsel must be actively sought at all stages. Furthermore, seeking multiple opinions from independent sources strengthens the reliability of the whole process, helping to prevent later disputes and ensure the agreement's protection of its signatories.

6.3 Dispute Resolution

Effective dispute resolution is paramount in safeguarding the integrity of a prenuptial agreement. Should disagreements arise concerning the interpretation or enforcement of the agreement, a well-defined dispute resolution process can prevent protracted and costly litigation, preserving the initial intent and protecting the financial well-being of both parties. A clearly outlined plan minimizes the potential for emotional distress and maintains a degree of civility during a potentially difficult time.

Negotiation remains the cornerstone of any effective dispute resolution strategy. Before resorting to more formal methods, encouraging open communication and mutual understanding between the parties involved is crucial. A successful negotiation hinges on a willingness to compromise and a collaborative approach focused on finding solutions that address each party's concerns fairly. It's advisable to involve legal counsel to guide the discussions and ensure all agreements reached reflect an accurate understanding of the legal implications involved. Remember, a well-structured agreement anticipates the possibility of future conflicts, mitigating their potential impact.

Mediation offers a less adversarial alternative to litigation. A neutral third party, typically a trained mediator experienced in family law, facilitates communication and helps guide the parties towards a mutually agreeable resolution. Mediation empowers the individuals involved to retain control over the outcome, unlike court proceedings, where a judge makes the final decisions. The confidential nature of mediation fosters a more open and productive environment, promoting creative solutions that may not be apparent in a formal legal setting. The mediator's role is to guide, not decide; they help bridge the gap between differing perspectives.

Arbitration provides a more formal, yet still less expensive and time-consuming alternative to court litigation. Here, a neutral arbitrator hears evidence and arguments from both sides before rendering a binding decision. While the arbitrator's decision is legally enforceable, the process maintains more flexibility than a court case, allowing for a greater degree of control over the proceedings and potential outcomes. Choosing an arbitrator experienced in family law and prenuptial agreements is paramount to a fair and informed decision. Unlike court, the parties often have more say in the selection of the arbitrator.

Litigation, the most formal and potentially costly method, should be considered a last resort. Court proceedings are expensive, time-consuming, and emotionally draining. However, it's a necessary option when mediation and arbitration fail to produce a satisfactory resolution. Legal representation is essential in litigation, as navigating the complexities of court procedures requires specialized legal knowledge. The court will apply relevant laws to the facts presented to arrive at a legally binding ruling. Understanding the likely outcomes and associated costs is crucial in determining whether litigation is a viable strategy.

Choosing an appropriate dispute resolution method depends on several factors, including the nature of the dispute, the complexity of the issues involved, the financial resources of the parties, and their level of comfort with each method. A well-drafted prenuptial agreement should explicitly outline the preferred method of dispute resolution, and it is recommended that both parties carefully consider their options and seek legal advice before making a decision. This preemptive measure clarifies expectations and helps maintain control over the process. The key is to select a mechanism appropriate for the situation, minimizing stress and ensuring fair outcomes.

Regardless of the chosen method, meticulous documentation throughout the entire process is crucial. Maintaining thorough records of all communications, agreements, and decisions helps ensure clarity and provides evidence should further action become necessary. This documentation serves as a critical reference point if the initial resolution needs revisiting or if any disputes arise concerning the implementation of agreed terms. The comprehensive documentation safeguards the rights and interests of both parties involved.

Effective dispute resolution, incorporated into a well-constructed prenuptial agreement, is a crucial preventative measure, promoting a greater likelihood of preserving the financial stability and emotional well-being of both parties. Proactive measures, such as a clearly defined dispute resolution clause and the guidance of legal counsel, can significantly reduce the chances of conflict escalating into protracted and expensive legal battles. In essence, prioritizing a robust dispute resolution plan is an investment in the long-term success of the prenuptial agreement itself. The peace of mind it offers significantly outweighs the initial effort invested in its creation.

7 Review & Updates

Life changes. Unexpected job losses, lucrative business ventures, inheritances, and even simple shifts in financial priorities can significantly alter the landscape of a pre-nuptial agreement. What was once a carefully crafted document reflecting your joint financial picture might become outdated, leaving your assets vulnerable. Ignoring this evolution is a serious oversight.

Regular reviews are not merely a good idea; they're a vital part of safeguarding the agreement's effectiveness. Consider it preventative maintenance for your financial future. Think of your pre-nup not as a static document signed and forgotten, but as a dynamic instrument that evolves alongside your life. Annual reviews, or at least every three years, are strongly recommended. Significant life events, such as the birth of a child, a change of employment, or a large inheritance, immediately necessitate review.

Amendments and modifications are the tools to keep your pre-nup aligned with reality. These alterations should be formalized, following the same legal procedures as the original agreement's creation. This is not a casual process; it needs legal counsel. Failing to do so can invalidate portions of the agreement, undermining its protective function, and opening the door to potential disputes during separation or divorce.

The process itself is usually straightforward. Both parties need to agree on the changes. Then, you engage your legal representative to draft the amendments, incorporating them clearly and precisely into the original agreement. These updated clauses are then signed and dated by both parties, with any witnesses, notary, or legal requirements fulfilled as per your jurisdiction's laws.

Don't underestimate the importance of clear and concise language. Ambiguity is the enemy of a robust pre-nup. Each amendment should be specifically worded to avoid any chance of misinterpretation. This clarity helps prevent later disputes about the intention and meaning of the changes. Consider having an attorney review the amendments before you sign them, to ensure legal soundness and alignment with your overall goals.

Failing to update your pre-nuptial agreement can result in significant financial consequences. A situation where one spouse's income has significantly increased and another's has stagnated could create an imbalance that wasn't initially foreseen. Similarly, unexpected debt or the acquisition of substantial assets can severely affect the fairness and efficacy of the original agreement. The agreement might no longer protect the interests of either spouse as intended.

Transparency remains paramount throughout this process. Open communication between you and your spouse is critical for a successful amendment. Understand each other's financial objectives and concerns. This collaborative approach will help ensure that the revised agreement continues to reflect your shared understanding and goals, preventing future conflict. Moreover, actively engaging in the review process demonstrates a willingness to work together, fostering stability within the marriage.

Remember, the goal isn't merely to protect assets; it is also to maintain a healthy and productive financial partnership. A well-maintained pre-nuptial agreement that reflects the evolution of your lives reduces conflict and fosters financial clarity, creating a stronger foundation for your marriage. Consider it an investment, not an expense, safeguarding both your present and future well-being. Regular review isn't just about legal compliance; it's about actively preserving the integrity of your agreement and the financial stability of your relationship.

7.1 Periodic Review

Life changes. Relationships evolve. Financial landscapes shift dramatically. What was meticulously crafted as a comprehensive pre-nuptial agreement five years ago might bear little resemblance to your current reality. This is precisely why regular review—a periodic, thorough examination—is not just advisable, it's crucial. Neglecting this process risks rendering your carefully constructed protection obsolete, leaving you vulnerable to unforeseen financial consequences should your marriage dissolve.

A simple annual review isn't sufficient. Significant life events demand immediate attention. A promotion, an inheritance, a substantial business transaction, or even the purchase of a significant asset like a home—all these necessitate a prompt reassessment of the agreement's provisions to ensure they accurately reflect your current financial position. Delaying this review increases the potential for legal complications and disputes later.

Your initial pre-nuptial agreement, while robust, was a snapshot in time. It documented your assets and liabilities at a specific point. The agreement likely outlined provisions for spousal support, property division, and debt allocation based on that snapshot. Now, you need a mechanism to update that snapshot. Consider the implications of a substantial investment that significantly alters your net worth or a significant increase in debt. Failure to account for these shifts can render certain clauses ineffective or, worse, unfair.

Think of your pre-nuptial agreement as a living document. It's not a static contract; it's a dynamic tool that requires regular maintenance to remain effective. This doesn't mean you need to completely rewrite the agreement every year. Rather, it involves a systematic process of review and adjustment. You might only need minor tweaks to reflect changes in asset values or addresses. Other times, more significant modifications might be necessary. This regular review process should involve both parties and ideally, their respective legal counsel to ensure all clauses remain legally sound and equitable.

The process itself shouldn't be daunting. Begin by gathering all relevant financial documentation: bank statements, investment portfolios, tax returns, property deeds, and any other paperwork that reflects your current financial state. Compare this new data against the original agreement's asset schedules and provisions. Look for discrepancies. Has the value of your home appreciated significantly? Have you incurred new debts? Has your income increased or decreased? Have significant assets been acquired since the signing of the agreement, such as through inheritance or a successful business venture? These are all crucial questions that need to be addressed during the review.

Documenting these changes is vital. Maintain a record of all amendments. Keep detailed notes of the review process, including the date, the specific changes made, and the reasons for those modifications. This meticulous record-keeping is not just prudent; it is essential for legal protection should any disputes arise in the future. Remember, transparency is paramount. Both parties must be fully informed of all changes made.

Beyond simply updating asset values, consider the bigger picture. Has your relationship dynamic changed? Have your individual life goals evolved? While a pre-nuptial agreement primarily deals with financial matters, it's important to acknowledge that substantial shifts in your personal circumstances can influence the agreement's relevance. For example, having children significantly alters the financial implications of separation or divorce. These emotional and relational factors, while not directly addressed in the financial components, are often integral to the future negotiations. These less quantifiable factors should also be considered when revisiting your agreement. It may prompt a conversation, not necessarily a rewrite, but a thoughtful consideration for future possibilities.

Remember that seeking legal counsel is not just recommended; it's essential. Attorneys specializing in family law can provide guidance on the necessary modifications and ensure that your agreement remains legally sound and enforceable. They can offer valuable insights into the potential impact of these changes, helping you make informed decisions that protect your interests. The cost of professional legal advice is a small price to pay for the peace of mind it provides, safeguarding against potential future disputes. Think of it as an investment in your long-term financial security. Ultimately, the goal is to maintain a pre-nuptial agreement that accurately reflects your current circumstances and continues to provide the protection and security you intended. Regular reviews, coupled with professional legal advice, are indispensable in achieving this.

7.2 Amendments & Modifications

Life changes. Circumstances shift. A pre-nuptial agreement, while meticulously crafted at its inception, isn't a static document; it's a living agreement that needs periodic attention to reflect the evolving realities of a marriage. This chapter details how to make those necessary amendments and modifications, ensuring your agreement remains a robust protector of your financial well-being.

Amendments and modifications to a pre-nuptial agreement require careful consideration and adherence to specific legal processes. Unlike casually altering a contract, a pre-nuptial agreement modification typically demands mutual consent and, in some jurisdictions, formal legal procedures. This isn't a process to be undertaken lightly or without professional legal guidance. Ignoring the legal formalities

could jeopardize the entire agreement's validity.
Significant life events often trigger the need for changes. A substantial inheritance, a major career advancement, the purchase of a new home, or even a considerable debt incurred during the marriage—these all warrant reviewing the existing provisions to maintain their effectiveness. Failing to account for these shifts might leave one party vulnerable to unforeseen financial repercussions should the marriage dissolve. For example, if one spouse receives a large inheritance after the pre-nup was signed, the agreement might need amending to reflect the increased asset pool and its implications for property division.
The process of amendment typically involves both spouses agreeing to the changes. This agreement should be documented formally, ideally in writing, outlining precisely the modifications being made to the original agreement. This written amendment should be signed by both parties, often witnessed and notarized, depending on your jurisdiction's legal stipulations. Remember, verbal agreements are precarious; written documentation provides a robust legal record.
Think of the original pre-nuptial agreement as a foundational blueprint. Amendments act as architectural additions, expansions, and sometimes even renovations that preserve the integrity of the original structure, while adding newer elements that respond to changed circumstances. This ensures your protection is not only comprehensive but also current.
Moreover, the complexities of state laws often influence the amendment process. Some states have specific requirements for modifying prenuptial agreements, including the necessity for independent legal counsel for each spouse. You must navigate these complexities with skilled legal guidance. Attempting to amend the agreement without proper legal counsel can lead to invalid modifications, or even worse, invalidate the entire agreement.
Beyond specific events, periodic reviews are crucial for maintain-

ing the agreement's relevance. Even in the absence of dramatic life changes, a regular review (every three to five years, or as advised by your legal counsel) is prudent. Market fluctuations, changes in tax laws, and unforeseen financial shifts all impact the agreement's effectiveness.

Consider this scenario: A couple establishes a pre-nup that equitably divides assets based on their initial financial positions. Five years later, one spouse experiences significant career growth, substantially increasing their net worth. The agreement needs revising to reflect this new reality, ensuring fairness and preventing potential disputes in the future. Without periodic reviews, such disparities can create imbalances, potentially undermining the very purpose of the pre-nuptial agreement itself.

Legal counsel is essential throughout the entire process. Amendments require a clear understanding of the original agreement's terms, applicable state laws, and the impact of the proposed modifications. An attorney specializing in family law can provide guidance through each step, ensuring the amendment is legally sound and protects your interests. They can also explain potential pitfalls and guide you toward solutions that maintain a fair and equitable agreement.

Therefore, remember that a pre-nuptial agreement is not a "set it and forget it" document. It's a dynamic instrument requiring periodic review and proactive amendment. By understanding the process and seeking professional legal advice, you can ensure your pre-nuptial agreement continues to effectively safeguard your assets and secure your financial future throughout your marriage, regardless of how life's circumstances may change. This proactive approach fosters financial security and protects your interests in the event of a future separation or divorce.

www.ingramcontent.com/pod-product-compliance
Ingram Content Group UK Ltd.
Pitfield, Milton Keynes, MK11 3LW, UK
UKHW020937290925
8121UKWH00041B/798

9 798349 265662